EXODUS 19-40

THE SHADOW OF GLORY

7 INTERACTIVE BIBLE STUDIES FOR SMALL GROUPS AND INDIVIDUALS

ANDREW REID

matthiasmedia

CW01582319

The Shadow of Glory
© Matthias Media 2008

Matthias Media
(St Matthias Press Ltd ACN 067 558 365)
PO Box 225
Kingsford NSW 2032
Australia
Telephone: (02) 9663 1478; international: +61-2-9663-1478
Facsimile: (02) 9663 3265; international: +61-2-9663-3265
Email: info@matthiasmedia.com.au
Internet: www.matthiasmedia.com.au

Matthias Media (USA)
Telephone: 724 964 8152; international: +1-724-964-8152
Facsimile: 724 964 8166; international: +1-724-964-8166
Email: sales@matthiasmedia.com
Internet: www.matthiasmedia.com

Unless otherwise indicated, all Scripture quotations are from The Holy Bible, English Standard Version, copyright © 2001 by Crossway Bibles, a publishing ministry of Good News Publishers. Used by permission. All rights reserved.

ISBN 978 1 921441 11 0

All rights reserved. Except as may be permitted by the Copyright Act, no part of this publication may be reproduced in any form or by any means without prior permission from the publisher.

Cover design and typesetting by Lankshear Design Pty Ltd.

» CONTENTS

» HOW TO MAKE THE MOST OF THESE STUDIES

1. What is an Interactive Bible Study?

Interactive Bible Studies are a bit like a guided tour of a famous city. They take you through a particular part of the Bible, helping you to know where to start, pointing out things along the way, suggesting avenues for further exploration, and making sure that you know how to get home. Like any good tour, the real purpose is to allow you to go exploring for yourself—to dive in, have a good look around, and discover for yourself the riches that God's word has in store.

In other words, these studies aim to provide stimulation and input and point you in the right direction, while leaving you to do plenty of the exploration and discovery yourself.

We hope that these studies will stimulate lots of 'interaction'—interaction with the Bible, with the things we've written, with your own current thoughts and attitudes, with other people as you discuss them, and with God as you talk to him about it all.

2. The format

Each study contains five main components:

- short sections of text that introduce, inform, summarize and challenge
- a set of numbered study questions that help you examine the passage and think through its meaning
- side-bars that provide extra bits of background or optional extra study ideas, especially regarding other relevant parts of the Bible
- an 'Implications' section that helps you think about what this passage means for you and your life today
- suggestions for thanksgiving and prayer as you close.

3. How to use these studies on your own

- Before you begin, pray that God would open your eyes to what he is saying in the Bible, and give you the spiritual strength to do something about it.
- Work through the study, reading the text, answering the questions about the Bible passage, and exploring the side-bars as you have time.
- Resist the temptation to skip over the 'Implications' and 'Give thanks and pray' sections at the end. It is important that we not only hear and understand God's word, but respond to it. These closing sections help us do that.
- Take what opportunities you can to talk to others about what you've learnt.

4. How to use these studies in a small group

- Much of the above applies to group study as well. The studies are suitable for structured Bible study or cell groups, as well as for more informal pairs and triplets. Get together with a friend or friends and work through them at your own pace; use them as the basis for regular Bible study with your spouse. You don't need the formal structure of a 'group' to gain maximum benefit.

- For small groups, it is *very useful* if group members can work through the study themselves *before* the group meets. The group discussion can take place comfortably in an hour (depending on how sidetracked you get!) if all the members have done some work in advance.
- The role of the group leader is to direct the course of the discussion and to try to draw the threads together at the end. This will mean a little extra preparation—underlining the sections of text to emphasize and read out loud, working out which questions are worth concentrating on, and being sure of the main thrust of the study. Leaders will also probably want to work out approximately how long they'd like to spend on each part.
- If your group members usually don't work through the study in advance, it's extra important that the leader prepares which parts to concentrate on, and which parts to glide past more quickly. In particular, the leader will need to select which of the 'Implications' to focus on.
- We haven't included an 'answer guide' to the questions in the studies. This is a deliberate move. We want to give you a guided tour of the Bible, not a lecture. There is more than enough in the text we have written and the questions we have asked to point you in what we think is the right direction. The rest is up to you.

5. Bible translation

Previous studies in our Interactive Bible Study series have assumed that most readers would be using the New International Version of the Bible. However, since the release of the English Standard Version in 2001, many have switched to the ESV for study purposes. For this reason, we have decided to quote from and refer to the ESV text, which we recommend.

» STUDY 1

BIRTH OF A NATION

[EXODUS 19]

A pivotal moment

IMAGINE THAT YOU WERE asked to pick the ten most significant moments or Bible passages in the history of God's people in the Old and New Testaments. What would they be?

Surely Genesis 1-3 would be in, because of its story of God the Creator and of humanity's bid for independence from him. Another would have to be God's promise to Abraham in Genesis 12, and the covenant that God makes with him in Genesis 15 and 17. You would almost certainly include the covenant with David in 2 Samuel 7, and you would not want to overlook the description of the sins of the kings and people of Israel and Judah in 2 Kings 17. But close to the top of your list, possibly inside the top three, would have to be Exodus 19-20, which we are now about to turn to. These chapters are pivotal both in the book of Exodus and within the Bible as a whole, because they look back on what has happened between God and his people, and they describe how their relationship will be shaped in the future.

Before we look at these chapters, it will be helpful to review just what has happened within Exodus to this point.

Which comes first: grace or law?

From this point on in the book of Exodus, much emphasis is given to laws and regulations of various sorts. One danger in reading these laws out of context is that we also get them out of perspective. We need to keep reminding ourselves that God's grace—his undeserved generosity—comes before God's law. So God *graciously* chose Abraham (Gen 12:1-3) and formed a covenant with him. Then God *graciously* heard his people's cry for help and remembered his covenant

The previous book, Genesis, finished with the people of God in Egypt. They were relatively small in number but were safe and secure under the leadership and protection of Joseph. By the beginning of Exodus, they had greatly increased in number but were slaves under the fierce oppression of an antagonistic Pharaoh, king of Egypt. Under his oppression they cried out to God (Exod 2:23-25). God heard them and rescued them through a series of plagues. Despite the spectacular nature of this deliverance, the people quickly forgot God's generosity, and spent their time grumbling and complaining on their way to Mt Sinai (Exod 15:22-18:27).

Now, three months after the exodus from Egypt, at the point where we pick up the story, they have arrived at the foot of Mt Sinai (Exod 19:1-2). They will stay there for about a year—that is, until Numbers 10:11-12.

(Exod 2:23-25). Then he *graciously* stretched out his hand to save his people. *All of this grace* preceded his giving of the law to Israel, and his calling on them to obey it. We mustn't let this focus on grace slip out of our minds as we spend our time examining God's law. It will help us understand what law is.

Covenants

Today the word 'covenant' is a legal expression, meaning a 'contract'. It has a legal dimension in the Bible too, but we should note that, fundamentally, 'covenant' language is the language of relationship. It conveys the idea of commitment in relationship, often involving mutual obligations and promises by one or both sides of the relationship. While there are covenants between individuals and nations described in the Old Testament, the majority of the references are to God's covenant with people. Already in the Old Testament, we've seen the covenant with Noah (Gen 9) and Abraham (Gen 12, 15, 17). It appears that the covenant referred to in verse 5 is seen as a development or continuation of the covenant with Abraham (cf. Exod 2:23-25).

Read Exodus 19:1-6.

These verses record God's foundational statements about how he understands his **covenant** (19:5) with Israel.

1. Who took the initiative in this covenant (v. 4)?

2. How did he show his initiative (v. 4)?

3. What response does God require to his initiative (v. 5)?

4. In response to Israel's response, what does God promise he will do for them (v. 6)?

5. Who else will benefit from all of this (v. 6)? (Hint: a priest is a mediator or a go-between; whom are they mediating between here?)

Thinking about priests

PRIESTS HAVE A NUMBER OF characteristics and roles in the Old Testament. They are set apart as devoted to God (Lev 21). They are to declare God's will to people (e.g. Lev 10:10-11; Deut 33:8-11; Jer 18:18; Hos 4:6), and to pray for people and offer sacrifices for them (Lev 9, 16). The whole world is God's, and Israel is to do these things for the people of his world (Gen 12:3; Deut 4:5-8).

Read Exodus 19:7–25.

6. How do God's people respond to his outline of the covenant (vv. 7-8)?

7. In this passage God promises to reveal himself.

a. Why does he make the promise to reveal himself?

b. Why do you think this might be important (v. 9)?

8. From God's instructions and his revelation of himself in verses 10-25, write down two or three words that summarize what you learn about God's nature.

9. If you had been present among the people at the base of Mt Sinai on that day, describe how you might have felt.

Thinking things through biblically

One of the striking things about this passage is the readiness of God's people to embrace the covenant and to pledge, "All that the Lord[1] has spoken we will do". The fickleness of Israel in the wilderness already leads us to wonder about their confidence. Their subsequent history, especially the incident of the golden calf in chapter 32, will demonstrate that they are overconfident. In Joshua 24:19, Joshua will be far more pessimistic. There the people will sound just as confident as God's people here, but Joshua will reply to them with these words: "You are not able to serve the Lord, for he is a holy God". So this leaves us with two problems. Given Israel's impending failure, who will fulfil the charter outlined for Israel here? And how can Israel have a future as God's people?

Fortunately, the Bible does not leave us with these terrifying questions unaddressed. First, it tells us that Jesus was able to do what Israel could not do. He was the ideal Son of God who was obedient to God and therefore functioned as a light to the nations (Luke 2:32; cf. Isa 42:6, 49:6, 51:4). Second, he was the means by whom God would deal with sin, so that it would not be remembered and human hearts would be transformed (e.g. Deut 30:6; Jer 31:31-34; Ezek 36:16-36). We know from the New Testament that God did this through the death of Jesus and the work of his Spirit (Rom 3:21-31, 8:1-17).

The point is that because humans are made of the same stuff as Adam and Eve, there is no hope for humanity if left on its own. Thankfully, God does not leave us on our own!

» Implications

Read 1 Peter 2:9-12.

- This passage describes the role of Christians in the world. How is the language similar to that of Exodus 19:3-6?

- According to this passage, what function do Christians have in the world?

- How is our function similar to that of Old Testament Israel in the world? How is it different?

- How well is your particular expression of the people of God (church, Bible study, etc.) fulfilling your God-ordained role, as described in this passage?

» Give thanks and pray

- Thank God for what he accomplished through Jesus in:
  - fulfilling the task that Israel failed to achieve
  - achieving forgiveness, the changing of human hearts, and the sending of the Spirit by his obedience to God.
- Pray that we will be effective, as God's people in his world, in our priestly role of declaring his great deeds and living godly lives among those who don't know him.

Endnote

1. In most English translations of the Bible, the word 'LORD' in capital letters means God's personal name, 'Yahweh' or 'I am who I am' (or possibly 'I will be who I will be'; see Exodus 3:13-14). We will follow this convention, where relevant, in these studies.

» STUDY 2

THE GIFT OF THE LAW

[Exodus 20]

What is 'law'?

When you hear the word 'law', what do you think? Perhaps you think of speed laws, or tax laws, or other sets of laws that operate in modern society. Such laws often have governments behind them, and authorities such as police to enforce them.

It is because we think this way that we often don't quite understand the Hebrew concept of law. The Hebrew word for 'law' is *torah*, and it is likely that it is derived from a word that has the sense of 'pointing the way', which in turn gives rise to the meaning 'direction', 'instruction' and 'teaching'. 'Law' in the Old Testament is not law in our sense, but rather direction or instruction or guidance about how people should conduct their lives.

The second thing to notice about Old Testament law was mentioned in the last study. Law flows out of relationship. Remember that before God urges people to obey in Exodus 19, he reminds them that he has borne them on eagle's wings and brought them to himself (19:4). He has acted to save them. It is as saved people that they are called upon to obey. They don't obey in order to enter relationship with God, but because they already are in relationship!

With all of this in mind, let us now look at Exodus 20. We will approach this not by looking at each commandment in detail, but rather by means of a broad overview.

Read Exodus 20:1-17.

Read verses 1-2 again. Did you notice that God reminds them again that the commandments arise out of a relationship formed by his rescue of them? That's the gracious context for everything that follows.

1. In the table below, all ten commandments are listed.[1]

a. Tick whether you think that they are primarily directed toward relating to God or relating to other people.

	Verses	Relating to God	Relating to other people
1	20:3		
2	20:4-6		
3	20:7		
4	20:8-11		
5	20:12		
6	20:13		
7	20:14		
8	20:15		
9	20:16		
10	20:17		

b. What do you think God might be saying to his people through this double focus in the commandments?

c. Do you think there is any similarity between the first commandment concerning relationship with God and the first one concerning relationship with others? What is it?

d. Read Matthew 22:34-40. How does what Jesus says fit in with the very structure of the ten commandments?

2. One good way of summarizing what the commandments are about is to say that they prohibit taking away something that belongs either to God or your neighbour. Try filling the table below with this in mind (a couple are filled in to give you a start).

	Verses	**Who is being deprived of something?**	**What are they being deprived of?**
1	20:3	God	Exclusive allegiance from his people.
2	20:4-6		
3	20:7		
4	20:8-11		
5	20:12	Neighbour	His life!
6	20:13		
7	20:14		
8	20:15		
9	20:16		
10	20:17		

3. Yet another good way to think about the commandments is that they are a reflection of the character of the God who gives them. What are some of the things that you learn about God from these commandments?

Thinking about the commandments

Can you see what is going on here? The more we look at them, the more we start to see that the ten commandments are about basic attitudes and principles in relating to God and neighbour—far more so than being 'laws' in our normal understanding of that word. This is particularly evident in two ways. First, the last commandment concerning **covetousness** is not something that you can bring to a law court for trial. Second, no penalties are prescribed for failure to keep them.

The ten commandments are a sort of summary of the central theological and ethical principles of the Old Testament. In this sense, they are general guidance or instruction. Other parts of the Old Testament will then show how such guidance works out in specific situations.

Coveting and the Sermon on the Mount

When we read the Sermon on the Mount in Matthew 5-7, we often think that Jesus is reinterpreting the commandments and pushing them further than just surface obedience. However, the tenth commandment about coveting indicates what is implicit in the rest of the commandments—that is, that attitudes of the heart and intentions lie under much of human sin. Hence, Jesus can tell us that murder and adultery are committed on the tongue or in the heart long before they are committed with weapons or in bed. Jesus is not *re*interpreting; he is simply explaining what is already there in the original commandments.

Read Exodus 20:18-26.

Verses 19 and 22 seem to indicate that the people had heard God speak the words of verses 2-17.

4. What emotional response do they have?

5. What is God's purpose in causing this response?

6. What do the people propose as a way forward?

» Implications

Let's see if we can summarize some of what we have learnt about the commandments and their implications. This is not the sum total of what there is to learn about law and faith. There is more to come in our following studies, but this is a good start.

- Who are the ten commandments for? (Remember, law flows from relationship!)

- The people of Israel are to keep the ten commandments.
    - Why should they do this?
    - What should be their attitude to the commandments?

Mediators and God

Have you ever wondered where the idea of Jesus as mediator comes from? It seems that it has its beginning in this chapter. The people here seek to protect themselves from God by having Moses stand in between them and God (perhaps fulfilling God's intention; 19:9). From now on, God will operate through mediators, with the ultimate mediator being Jesus (cf. 1 Tim 2:5; Heb 8:6, 9:15, 12:24). It's also worth noting that this makes the ten commandments very distinctive: they are the *only* unmediated commands from God to Israel.

The ten commandments in the New Testament

The New Testament mentions the commandments in a number of places. We've already noted the Sermon on the Mount. Some others include Matthew 19:16-19, Mark 10:17-20 and Romans 13:9-10. Can you think of other references, perhaps to individual commandments?

- Should Christians keep all the commandments? Why? Why not?

- Should those who are not Christians be told to keep the commandments? What might be the impact of telling people who are not related to God that they should keep the commandments?

» Give thanks and pray

- Thank God for the new covenant that he has instituted with us through Jesus.
- Pray that we might rightly respond to this covenant by acting in ways that please God. In particular, pray that God might help us to love him with all our heart, soul, and mind; and to love our neighbour as ourselves.
- Pray for the group of Christians that you meet with regularly, that you might be known, as individuals and as a group, by your love of God and love of neighbour.

Endnote

1. There is some debate as to how the commandments should be divided. The traditional break-up is given here.

» STUDY 3

A DELIGHTFUL LAW

[Exodus 20:22-23:19]

Delighting in law

ARE YOU LIKE MANY MODERN Christians when you read Old Testament law? Do you find it a bit like reading genealogies, or worse, like skimming through a phone book? Is it boring or tedious and burdensome? Perhaps you might even be more negative than this, and consider Old Testament law to be outdated and irrelevant now that you've come to know Christ.

In the chapters we are going to look at in this study, the focus is on law. As we look at these laws, we need to understand the Israelite mentality. You see, the true Israelite loved law because he understood it to be a gracious expression of the mind, heart and character of the God who had redeemed him, and whom he worshipped. It was also the way God had provided for his people to gratefully respond to him. This attitude is captured in Psalm 119, which speaks about God's law as a delight, and a basis for true meditation. It was so full of wonderful things that souls were consumed with longing for it. It supplied strength for the weary and refreshment for the spiritually dry. Rather than being a source of death, it was the ground of life itself (Deut 32:47).

Before we launch into this section, let's remember what we have learnt so far:

- Law is a reflection of relationship. God acted in grace and formed a relationship with his people. That relationship is the background and precursor to law. Law flows from grace—not vice versa.

- Old Testament law flows in two directions: relationship with God and relationship with other people. It can be summarized in the commands to love God and to love your neighbour.
- The term 'law' means 'instruction' or 'teaching' or 'guidance'. This means that we shouldn't expect Old Testament law to cover every situation. The Old Testament laws are illustrations of how love of God and love of neighbour can be expressed. There are many other contexts and ways in which God's love might be expressed.

Read Exodus 21:1-36.

There are other types of legal material but two common types are 'case' law and 'apodictic' law.

1. 'Case law' is generally when you have a law that addresses a certain case. It is conditional and is introduced by the words 'when' or 'if'. Find three examples of case law in the passage.

2. 'Apodictic law' or 'absolute law' is when the law has no conditions to it (e.g. the ten commandments). They can be positive ('Honour your father and mother') or negative ('You shall not steal'). Find three examples.

Exodus 21:1-23:19.

3. The laws cover many areas of life. Read the following passages and write down the areas of life that are covered (you may like to divide the passages between the group members). The first example has been provided.

- 21:2-11 Human rights (slaves, daughters)
- 21:12-15
- 21:18-25
- 22:7-15
- 22:16-17
- 22:19
- 22:29-30
- 23:6-9
- 23:10-12

4. In various places a basis or motivation is given for a law. What sort of basis is given in the following passages?

   - 20:8-11

   - 20:12

   - 21:8

   - 22:21

   - 23:8

Christians and Old Testament law

Our views on Old Testament law are significantly formed by what we read in the New Testament. However, often we don't get these passages in proper balance. Read the following passages and write down what is said about Old Testament law in the New Testament.

Passage	The law is ...
Matt 5:17-20	
Rom 5:20-21	
Rom 7:1-12	
Gal 3:19-26	
2 Tim 3:15-17	

Interpreting Old Testament law

When we read the passages just listed, they give us some boundaries for approaching Old Testament law.

First, law is part of Scripture, therefore it can teach us about Christ. Because it teaches us about Christ, it is therefore also able to make us wise for salvation, and teach us right doctrine and conduct.

Second, it is possible to abuse law by cutting it loose from its context of grace and turning it into a way of entering relationship with God. This must be avoided.

Third, Jesus fulfils the law. This doesn't mean that he does away with it, but that it can only be understood properly for us as Christian people in the light of what God has done in Jesus Christ.

There is much more that could be said, but the diagram below gives a way ahead for working out the implications of Old Testament law. First, when you read a particular law, separate the theological or ethical principles that undergird this law (e.g. treating disadvantaged people in society with proper care). Second, ask whether the coming of Christ has changed the implications of this law for Christians (e.g. food laws). Third, in the light of this, work out what the implications of this law are in your own context.

This could be summarized in the following illustration:[1]

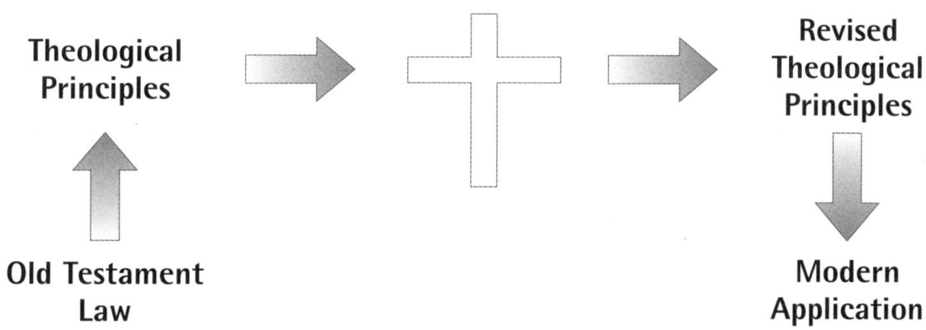

Here's another way of thinking about it. When you read Old Testament legal material, ask the following questions of it:

- What does this law tell us about God and relationship with him?
- What does it tell us about how to relate to other people?
- Does the life, death, and ministry of Jesus change what the Old Testament law taught?
- What are the implications of this for us as Christians in our situation?

» Implications

Take a small section of law (e.g. from the laws in Exodus 21-23) and work through one of the approaches outlined on the previous page.

» Give thanks and pray

- Take one of the sections of Psalm 119, and turn it into a prayer about God's law.

Endnote

1. Paul Barker, *Deuteronomy: The God Who Keeps Promises*, Acorn, Melbourne 1998, pp. 76-78. Reproduced with permission.

» STUDY 4

BLOOD AND EATING

[Exodus 23:20-24:18]

Promises and demands

We have travelled some distance now in the book of Exodus. We started with a group of people who were in covenant with God through Abraham, Isaac and Jacob. God heard their groaning, remembered his covenant (Exod 2:23-25), and came down to rescue them and bring them up out of Egypt (3:8). He has now entered into a covenant with those people, and they have embraced it. He has outlined to them some of its obligations in the form of commandments and judgements that will characterize their relationship with him and each other. In the next chapter, he will formalize that covenant. However, before he does this, he says three more things.

First, he promises present comfort for his people in the form of an angel who will guard them, bring them to the place God has prepared, speak to them, and punish them in the case of disobedience (23:20-21).

Second, God outlines his future actions. As he sends an angel in the present, so he will send terror and hornets in the future to prepare the land and its occupants for God's people (23:27-28). He will bless his people and drive out those who currently dwell there.

Third, he makes it clear that his great promises come with demands: avoid idolatry (23:24), and serve the real God instead (23:25). In other words, they are to give God their devotion and worship.

Exodus 19 and 24

Exodus 19 and 24 are closely linked. Exodus 19 begins the section on the covenant with God revealing himself and declaring the covenant. Exodus 24 records him establishing or ratifying it. In the original language, both chapters have seven references to God speaking, or to God's word. Chapter 19 has seven references to 'going down', while chapter 24 has seven references to 'going up'. In other words, the content and structure of these chapters indicate that they are to be read in the light of each other. Taken together, Exodus 19 and 24 describe God's formalizing of his relationship with his people. Originally God had enacted his covenant with Abraham personally. Now God formalizes that covenant with the entire nation descended from Abraham.

Read Exodus 24.

1. Use the following chart to summarize what happens.

Verses	Events
1-2	The people ... Moses, Aaron, Nadab, Abihu, and the seventy elders ... Moses alone ...
3	Moses ... The people ...
4	Moses ... 1. 2.
5	Moses ...
6-7	Moses ... The people ... Moses ...
9-11	Moses, Aaron, Nadab, Abihu and the seventy elders ...
12-18	God instructs Moses to ... Moses (and Joshua) ...

2. Imagine the circle below represents the whole of Mt Sinai and its immediate vicinity. Draw the various places mentioned in this chapter, and write down on your diagram who is allowed to go where.

Thinking biblically

There are many useful ways in which we could think about this chapter within the context of the whole Bible. However, we will focus on just one in this study— the idea of 'eating with God'.

Read Isaiah 25:6-8.

3. Isaiah speaks of an end time mountain feast. What is striking about it when compared to the meal with God in Exodus 24? (Hint: Who is there?)

Read Hebrews 9:19-28.

Here the writer of Hebrews alludes to Exodus 24.

4. In what way does the blood in Exodus 24 foreshadow the work of Christ?

5. How is the blood of Christ different from the blood of the sacrifices in Exodus 24?

The blood rite

We're not explicitly told what the blood rite means in verses 3-8. However, there are a number of elements to note that can help us make a good guess:

- Israel agrees to all the terms of the covenant (vv. 3, 7).
- The altar symbolizes God, while the twelve pillars symbolize Israel (v. 4).
- Much blood is gathered from sacrifices (v. 5).
- Burnt offerings are generally connected with atonement for sin and consecration. Peace/fellowship offerings celebrate fellowship with God.
- The blood is splashed over the two covenant partners or the thing that symbolizes them (vv. 6, 8). This splashing may symbolize that:
  - the two parties are now bound together
  - this is only possible through a sacrifice of atonement.
- Only after this rite takes place can the representatives of Israel then do what happens in verses 9-11.

Read Hebrews 10:19-25.

6. What does the sacrifice of Christ achieve, and how is it similar to and different from what is achieved in Exodus 24?

» Implications

- What echoes of Exodus 24 are found in the Lord's Supper (cf. Luke 22:14-20)?

- What is so spectacular about the imagery of the Lord's Supper in the light of Exodus 24?

» Give thanks and pray

- Give thanks for the sacrifice of Christ, which gives us bold access to God.
- Pray that we might hold unswervingly to the hope we have in Christ, relying on the faithfulness of God.
- Pray that we might spur one another on to love and good deeds as we see the day of God approaching.

» STUDY 5

A SHADOW OF GLORY

[Exodus 25-31 and 35:1-40:33]

Do you remember the diagram that you drew for Exodus 24 in the previous study? The circle represented the mountain, and various people were allowed in various places—but only after certain things were done. In many ways, what we saw happening in chapter 24 was a blueprint for the tabernacle that will be outlined in the rest of the book of Exodus.

Approximately one third of the book of Exodus is about the tabernacle. For most modern readers, the space and detail given to the design and construction of the tabernacle is a bit overwhelming. However, there are some very important things being said. The amount of space given to it indicates that the author thought our time wouldn't be wasted in giving such details close attention.

To highlight the most important elements of these chapters, in this study we will:

- get the big picture of what happens
- understand the structure and function of the tabernacle
- work out the implications for our lives as Christians today.

Thinking about the Sabbath

Chapters 25-31 contain seven references containing statements such as, "The LORD said to Moses" or "The LORD spoke to Moses" (25:1, 30:11, 30:17, 30:22, 30:34, 31:1, 31:12). The first six of these references deal with creative acts and the seventh features a reference to the Sabbath, which is specifically grounded in creation. Moreover, the instructions about building the tabernacle *end* with the Sabbath (31:12-18), while the record of its construction *begins* with the Sabbath (35:1-3). Also, the words used of Moses finishing the work on the tabernacle in Exodus 40:33 have strong echoes of God finishing his work on the seventh day in Genesis 2:2.

The big picture

1. Most modern Bibles have headings for each major section. Skim through the headings for chapters 25-40 and summarize what each of the following sections is about:

   - chapters 25-31

   - chapters 32-34

   - chapters 35-40

2. Read Exodus 25:9 and 25:40. What do these verses tell us about the tabernacle?

Everything in its place

3. In the following diagram the main items of furniture for the tabernacle are identified with arrows and Bible references. Read at least one of the passages and write in the name of the item.

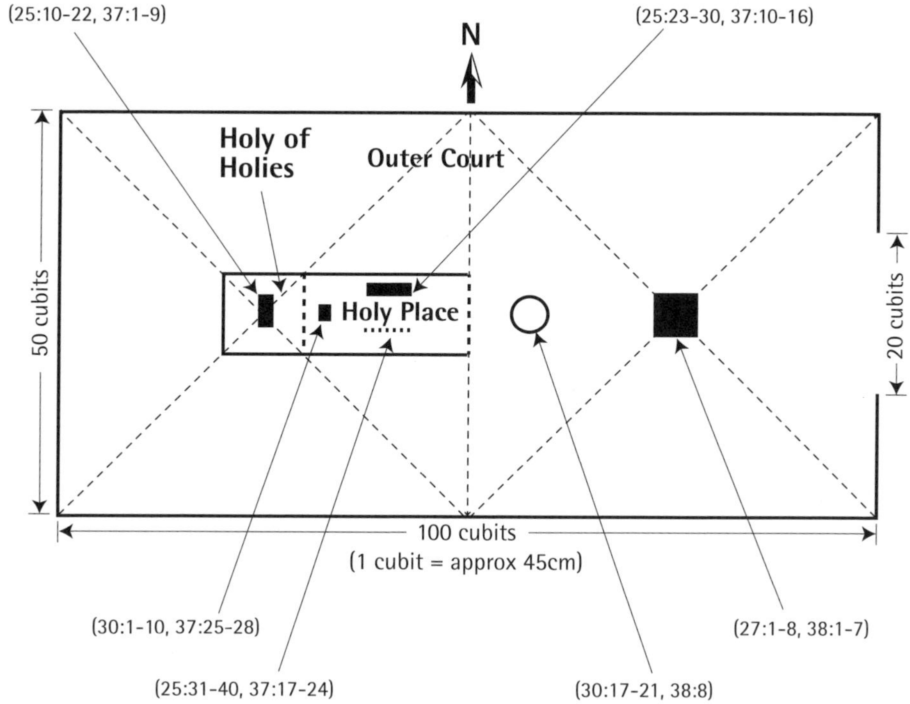

The function of the tabernacle

4. Read Exodus 25:8 and 40:34 and compare them with Psalm 103:19 and 1 Kings 8:27. What is the tabernacle, and what does it symbolize or say to God's people?

5. Think about the two halves of the book of Exodus. The first half tells us that God redeems his people *from* slavery. However, the second half tells us that God redeems his people *to* or *for* something. What is it that God redeems his people *to* or *for*?

6. Think about the allusions to creation and the Sabbath. By doing this, God is urging us to think back to Genesis 1-2, where God creates the world, declares it to be "very good", and places the pinnacle of his creation—Adam and Eve—in the garden of Eden as rulers over his world.

   a. In terms of God's relationship with humanity, what does the garden of Eden represent? (If necessary, go back to Genesis 1-2 and skim-read, looking especially for verses that describe the relationship God establishes with mankind.)

   b. What do you think God is doing by describing the tabernacle with this Genesis-type language?

The ark, cherubs and footstools

The top of the ark had a plate of gold. This was where the rites of the Day of Atonement were conducted (Lev 16), and therefore represented how God was present among his people to dispense mercy and forgiveness. At each end of the top of the ark there was a cherub whose wings stretched out, perhaps symbolizing a footstool (1 Chr 28:2; Ps 99:5, 132:7), above which was the divine throne itself.

Thinking biblically

Read John 1:14-18.

7. The words 'dwelt' or 'made his dwelling' in verse 14 might also be translated 'tabernacled'.[1] Notice also the word 'glory', which occurs in Exodus 29:43 and 40:34-35. What is John saying by making these links between Jesus and Exodus?

Read 1 Corinthians 3:16-17 and Ephesians 2:22.

8. God now has some new portable tabernacles or temples. What or who are they?

» Implications

- We Christians are the means of spreading the presence of God in the world. We do this by:
  - speaking the word of the gospel that brings people into relationship with God and into his presence as well
  - living for Christ in his world.

  How would your moral and spiritual life change if you took seriously the fact that God has chosen you as a place in which to dwell?

- Look at how Paul reflects on this in relation to one area of sin in 1 Corinthians 6:18-20.

» Give thanks and pray

- Give thanks that we can boldly enter God's presence in Christ.
- Pray for our role as God's presence in the world. In particular, pray together for friends or family who do not yet know Christ (if you are working on these studies in a group then you might share the name of these friends and continue to pray for them throughout these studies).

Endnote

1. There are links between the Greek word used in John 1:14 for 'dwelling' and that used for 'tabernacle' in the Greek version of the Old Testament.

» STUDY 6

GOD REPENTS

[Exodus 32]

THERE IS A SAD PATTERN THAT occurs often in Scripture. At a number of places we see God forge a new and wonderful stage in his relationship with his people. Then, within the space of a chapter or two, some of the same people who have been beneficiaries of God's grace fail in some particularly shameful way. For example, the rescue of Noah and his family in Genesis 6-9 is followed by the drunkenness of Noah and the dishonourable conduct of Ham (Gen 9:18-28). Or the promise by God to Abram in Genesis 12:1-3 is followed by Abram's deceitful conduct in Egypt, which results in Pharaoh's household being cursed rather than blessed by its encounter with Abram (Gen 12:10-20). God's promise to David in 2 Samuel 7 is shortly followed by the seduction (possibly even rape) of Bathsheba, and the murder of Uriah (2 Sam 11). It is as though God (through the writers of the narratives) is showing us that despite his grace to humans, they are still sinful and unable to rescue themselves.

We've already seen a little of this in Exodus. The great rescue of chapters 14-15 is followed by grumbling and lack of faith in chapters 15-17. Now, God's entering into covenant, and his granting of access to his presence through the tabernacle, is followed by an act of terrible unfaithfulness.

Read Exodus 32:1-6.

1. Give one word that might summarize the attitude of the people in verse 1.

Impatience
faithlessness
Slave mentality of Galatians 5:1
Aaron - fear. Of people, then of Moses

2. Read the first and second commandment again in Exodus 20:3-6. Which commandment do you think they are breaking here (note the reference to "the LORD" in verse 5)?

'besides'

3. The last time that the people of God offered peace/fellowship offerings and burnt offerings was Exodus 24:5. What accompanied those offerings in chapter 24, and what accompanies them here?

Is there anything wrong with feasting & revelling?
Ch. often accused of being killjoy...
(but 'play' suggests sexual licence)
Romans 1:24,25

Read Exodus 32:7-10.

4. During the rescue of his people out of Egypt, God has a particular way of referring to his people (e.g. Exod 3:7, 5:1, 9:1) and his actions on their behalf (Exod 13:14, 20:2). How does he turn this on its head in verse 7?

my people
your people

Read Exodus 3:7-10.

5. Look for the references to God 'seeing'. What does he see and how does he react? Now look at Exodus 32:9-10. What does God see now, and how will he react?

Read Exodus 2:23-25.

6. Comparing this passage with Exodus 32:7-10:

a. Why did God rescue Israel?

b. How is God threatening to go against this in Exodus 32:10, and how will he go about it?

God's change of mind

Various versions of the Bible use different words for one critical Hebrew word in 32:12 and 14 (e.g. ESV and NIV: 'relent'; NRSV and NASB: 'change mind'; RSV: 'repent'). The word is linked with regret and compassion. Moses is asking God to be so moved with pain that he reverses what he was going to do.

There are two comments to make. First, we must not try to dodge or fudge what is being said here. God is not presented as pretending in verses 7-11, nor is his change of mind presented as being anything less than exactly that in verse 14. This may raise some enormous questions. However, we are dealing with Scripture and we must not water it down. Our job, rather, is to work hard at understanding it.

Second, did you notice the wonderful interplay in this passage? In effect, verses 7-10 tell us that God threatened to change his mind regarding the promises to Abraham, by starting again with Moses. What Moses does is to ask God to change his mind regarding this change of mind by returning to his original intention. In effect he is asking God not to change his mind at all!

Read Exodus 32:11-14.

7. How does the basis of Moses' argument pick up some of God's comments in verses 7-10?

Read Exodus 32:15-35.

8. What did the stone tablets represent?

9. What, therefore, is being symbolized by Moses breaking them (v. 19)?

10. How does Moses attempt to make **atonement** (vv. 30-32), and what is God's response?

» Implications

- Do you remember how the tabernacle recalled Genesis 1-2? Now the golden calf incident recalls Genesis 3. What is the author telling us about human nature?

- Did you notice the urgency and boldness of Moses in prayer? He was not afraid to put things before God in a forthright manner, and to ask God to act in response. Many other people in the Bible pray this way. Is our view of God and of relationship with him such that we can pray with this level of boldness, urgency and intimacy? Talk about this amongst the group.

Mediators and substitutes

Moses performs the role of a mediator throughout this chapter and the next in a number of ways. However, he does suggest one mediatorial role that is refused by God: that of being a substitute—or making atonement for the sins of others—by offering himself.

Moses captures something that is later made very plain in the New Testament. He does not suggest sacrifices such as burnt offerings. Rather, he senses that human sin might need to be atoned for by the substitutionary death of a human. On the cross, Jesus does what God did not allow Moses to do here. The sinless Jesus took the place of sinful people so that we might be righteous before God, and not have to face the punishment due to us (2 Cor 5:21).

» Give thanks and pray

- What have you found surprising or confusing or new about God in this passage? Pray about these things. Pray that your knowledge of God will continue to deepen as you study his word.
- Thank God for Jesus, the one mediator between God and humanity. Thank God for his substitutionary death on our behalf.
- Given that our relationship with God is secure through Christ, we can be confident before him. Pray that your prayer life and that of your Christian friends might be characterized by a boldness and intimacy that reflects that relationship.

» STUDY 7

THE HOPE OF GLORY

[Exodus 33-34 and 40:34-38]

THE MOVIE *Signs* INVOLVES AN alien visitation of our planet. At the heart of the film is not an interest in aliens, but exploring the views of one man, an Episcopal clergyman who has lost his faith because of a car accident in which his wife was killed. In a poignant moment the brother of this clergyman asks for a word of comfort. The clergyman (played by Mel Gibson) talks about two groups of people. There are those who experience good things and ascribe it to "someone out there watching out for them", and those who see it as "just pure luck, a happy turn of chance". He observes that the second group are filled with fear when bad things threaten. Finally his brother asks which group he is in and Gibson's character says, "There is no one watching out for us, Merrill. We are all on our own."

It is a very sad moment in the film. For those who have believed or known God, there is nothing so crushing to the spirit than to come to the realization that either God is not there or he has withdrawn his presence. This is the situation that is being faced by the Israelites in Exodus 33. The covenant has been broken and Israel faces God's possible absence.

Read Exodus 33:1-6.

1. How is God's grace as well as his anger displayed in verses 1-3?

2. Why do you think that the ornaments are singled out for mention in verses 4-6 (cf. Exod 3:22, 12:36, 32:2-3)?

Read Exodus 33:7-23.

Remember that at this time the tabernacle and the ark had not yet been built. They are built in chapters 35-40. These verses therefore talk about the presence of God in this interim time.

3. What contrast is offered between Moses' experience of the presence of God and the experience of God's people as outlined in verses 1-6?

Can we really see God's glory?

VERSES 12-16 TAKE UP A NUMBER OF issues in what is quite a complicated interaction. Moses is basically asking two things. First, who exactly is going to be sent with him and the people (v. 12)? Second, what exactly is God going to do (v. 13: "show me now your ways")?

God's response is to tell Moses that God himself will be going with them (literally, 'my face'), albeit via the intermediary of the angel, and his purpose is to give rest in the land. The 'you' that is to be given rest in verse 14 is singular, which is probably why Moses stresses with God the importance of the people and not just himself in verses 15-16. God's people need God's presence. It is this alone that makes them distinctive.

God's response of assurance comes in verse 17, where he assures Moses that he will grant him his requests. Moses pushes further and poses a third request, to be shown God's glory!

In the Old Testament, God's glory is the thing that makes God 'shine'—the very thing that makes God 'God'. So Moses has indeed asked a very bold thing!

However, there is a limit to what Moses might see of God without risk to himself. The Lord's merciful yet gracious response is to tell Moses that his goodness will pass before him. God will shield him from the absolute glory of his presence.

Read Exodus 34:1-9.

4. List the things that Moses and the people are to do to prepare for God's revelation of himself and the renewal of the covenant.

5. There are seven words or phrases used to describe God in verses 6-7.

a. What are they?

b. Which ones concern his favourable disposition toward people?

Things to note about 34:6-7

It appears that what happens in these verses is what Moses asked for in chapter 33—that is, to understand God's ways and see his glory. Intriguingly, what we then have described is not a vision that can be seen, but words! These words describe God in terms of his name and character. God is known through his word. That is why both orthodox Jews and Christians spend so much time studying the Scriptures.

Some English translations simply have 'thousands' in verse 7. Others have 'thousands of generations'. The original Hebrew simply has 'thousands'. However, the translations that add 'of generations' are on the right track in comparing the thousands of generations to whom God shows steadfast love with the three or four generations on whom he visits iniquity (see Deut 7:9 where the Hebrew has the word 'generations'). God's mercy triumphs over his judgement.

c. Which ones have more negative connotations, and how are those connotations softened?

d. Write a one sentence summary of what you learn about the character of God from these verses.

Urging God to be God!

THE BOOK OF EXODUS HAS TOLD US that God promised an oath to Abraham, Isaac and Jacob. He promised to be their God, and the God of their descendants. God honoured his oath by rescuing his people out of Egypt, and extending his covenant with Abraham to the whole nation. In Exodus 24 that covenant is enacted.

However, in Exodus 32 the people of God break the covenant. At this point, God has every right to walk away from what he said he would do for the people he's chosen. But Moses intervenes and pleads with God to change his mind—which he does.

In Exodus 34, God urges Moses to prepare for the covenant tablets to be written up again. It is then that he reveals his character to Moses in verses 6-7. What he tells Moses is that he is a God whose overwhelming desire is to forgive, to have surprising mercy, love and kindness. In other words, when Moses pleads with God, he is pleading correctly. He is simply urging God to be the God that he is by inclination. This is why, when these verses are quoted later in the Old Testament, they often have an additional line added that says something along the lines of 'who relents from sending calamity' (e.g. Joel 2:13; Jonah 4:2). It is this in God that is behind him restoring the covenant in the subsequent verses of chapter 34.

Read Exodus 34:10-35.

6. Verses 10-28 renew the covenant by reiterating key elements. In the table below, write down which verses recall which elements.

The Passover	
The ten commandments	
The book of the covenant (i.e. the 'judgements' of chapters 21-23)	
The deliverance from Egypt (cf. 3:20, 15:1-10)	

7. What new emphasis is present (that takes into account the golden calf incident)?

8. How is the people's response to Moses different from when he was last on the mountain?

Read Exodus 40:34-38.

9. Given Exodus 32-33, what is striking about what happens here? How does it show that God is who he revealed himself to be in Exodus 34:6-7?

» Implications

- Read Romans 3:9-20, which summarizes Paul's argument about humanity in the section that has run from Romans 1:18. If humanity is like this, what should humans expect from God?

- Read Romans 3:21-26. How do God's actions show him to be the same God that we have seen in Exodus 32-34?

- Why not memorize Exodus 34:6-7? It is a wonderful description of God and his nature that leads us inevitably toward the work of Jesus on the cross.

- Note some of the ways in which Moses prefigures Christ in these chapters:
    - his offer of atonement
    - his mediatorial role (presenting God to the people and the people to God)
    - his intercession on behalf of the people.

  How is Jesus similar to, but also different from, Moses?

» Give thanks and pray

- Turn Exodus 34:6-7 into a prayer of thanks for who God is.
- Thank God that through Moses, we see more clearly the great mediator, priest, prophet, and leader of God's people—Jesus Christ.

Matthias Media is a ministry team of like-minded, evangelical Christians working together to achieve a particular goal, as summarized in our mission statement:

To serve our Lord Jesus Christ, and the growth of his gospel in the world, by producing and delivering high quality, Bible-based resources.

It was in 1988 that we first started pursuing this mission together, and in God's kindness we now have more than 250 different ministry resources being distributed all over the world. These resources range from Bible studies and books through to training courses and audio sermons.

To find out more about our large range of very useful products, and to access samples and free downloads, visit our website:

www.matthiasmedia.com.au

How to buy our resources

1. Direct from us over the internet:
   - in the US: www.matthiasmedia.com
   - in Australia and the rest of the world: www.matthiasmedia.com.au
2. Direct from us by phone:
   - in the US: 1 866 407 4530
   - in Australia: 1800 814 360 (Sydney: 9663 1478)
   - international: +61-2-9663-1478
3. Through a range of outlets in various parts of the world. Visit **www.matthiasmedia.com.au/international.php** for details about recommended retailers in your part of the world, including www.thegoodbook.co.uk in the United Kingdom.
4. Trade enquiries can be addressed to:
   - in the US: sales@matthiasmedia.com
   - in the UK: sales@ivpbooks.com
   - in Australia and the rest of the world: sales@matthiasmedia.com.au

Also from Matthias Media

Out of Darkness

Exodus 1-18

An oppressed people, a reluctant hero, a cruel and all-powerful dictator.

As the book of Exodus opens, we wonder how God is going to keep his ancient promises to his chosen people. But in his majestic power, God proves himself to be more than a match for Egypt's arrogant king. As God rescues his wayward people, and gathers them to himself at Mt Sinai, we see a stunning picture of God's grace and faithfulness and power and truth. Despite the obstacles, despite the seeming hopelessness of the situation, despite even the sinfulness of those needing rescue, God brings his people out of darkness and into his wonderful light.

In this series of eight studies on Exodus 1-18, Andrew Reid guides us through the extraordinary story of God's rescue of Israel, and shows us how this drama points to the work of Christ.

FOR MORE INFORMATION OR TO ORDER CONTACT:

Matthias Media
Telephone: +61-2-9663-1478
Facsimile: +61-2-9663-3265
Email: info@matthiasmedia.com.au
Internet: www.matthiasmedia.com.au

Matthias Media (USA)
Telephone: 1-866-407-4530
Facsimile: 724-964-8166
Email: sales@matthiasmedia.com
Internet: www.matthiasmedia.com

Also from Matthias Media

Full of Promise

The big picture of the Old Testament

- If you've always wondered what the Old Testament is really about ...
- If you feel like the Old Testament is a confusing mix of hard-to-understand laws and boring history ...
- If you've ever been confused about how the Old Testament relates to Jesus ...

... then you need *Full of Promise*.

In *Full of Promise*, Phil Campbell and Bryson Smith take us on an exciting tour of the Old Testament. In just eight studies, we see the big breathtaking picture of creation, the fall and the history of God's dealings with Israel—the whole story, with all its ups and downs, and with the certainty of God's promise shining through.

These invaluable studies help us to understand the message of the whole Bible. They show us not only the big picture of the Old Testament, but how the pieces fit together, and how they point to the One who was to come: Jesus, in whom all God's promises are Yes and Amen.

FOR MORE INFORMATION OR TO ORDER CONTACT:

Matthias Media
Telephone: +61-2-9663-1478
Facsimile: +61-2-9663-3265
Email: info@matthiasmedia.com.au
Internet: www.matthiasmedia.com.au

Matthias Media (USA)
Telephone: 1-866-407-4530
Facsimile: 724-964-8166
Email: sales@matthiasmedia.com
Internet: www.matthiasmedia.com

Other Interactive and Topical Bible Studies from Matthias Media

Our Interactive Bible Studies (IBS) and Topical Bible Studies (TBS) are a valuable resource to help you keep feeding from God's word. The IBS series works through passages and books of the Bible; the TBS series pulls together the Bible's teaching on topics such as money or prayer. As at July 2008, the series contains the following titles:

Beyond Eden
GENESIS 1-11
Authors: Phillip Jensen and Tony Payne, 9 studies

Out of Darkness
EXODUS 1-18
Author: Andrew Reid, 8 studies

The Shadow of Glory
EXODUS 19-40
Author: Andrew Reid, 7 studies

The One and Only
DEUTERONOMY
Author: Bryson Smith, 8 studies

The Good, the Bad and the Ugly
JUDGES
Author: Mark Baddeley, 10 studies

Famine and Fortune
RUTH
Authors: Barry Webb and David Höhne, 4 studies

Renovator's Dream
NEHEMIAH
Authors: Phil Campbell and Greg Clarke, 7 studies

The Eye of the Storm
JOB
Author: Bryson Smith, 6 studies

The Search for Meaning
ECCLESIASTES
Author: Tim McMahon, 9 studies

Two Cities
ISAIAH
Authors: Andrew Reid and Karen Morris, 9 studies

Kingdom of Dreams
DANIEL
Authors: Andrew Reid and Karen Morris, 9 studies

Burning Desire
OBADIAH AND MALACHI
Authors: Phillip Jensen and Richard Pulley, 6 studies

Warning Signs
JONAH
Author: Andrew Reid, 6 studies

Full of Promise
THE BIG PICTURE OF THE O.T.
Authors: Phil Campbell and Bryson Smith, 8 studies

The Good Living Guide
MATTHEW 5:1-12
Authors: Phillip Jensen and Tony Payne, 9 studies

News of the Hour
MARK
Author: Peter Bolt, 10 studies

Mission Unstoppable
ACTS
Author: Bryson Smith, 10 studies

The Free Gift of Life
ROMANS 1-5
Author: Gordon Cheng, 8 studies

The Free Gift of Sonship
ROMANS 6-11
Author: Gordon Cheng, 8 studies

Proclaiming the Risen Lord
LUKE 24-ACTS 2
Author: Peter Bolt, 6 studies

Free for All
GALATIANS
Authors: Phillip Jensen and Kel Richards, 8 studies

Walk this Way
EPHESIANS
Author: Bryson Smith, 8 studies

Partners for Life
PHILIPPIANS
Author: Tim Thorburn, 8 studies

The Complete Christian
COLOSSIANS
Authors: Phillip Jensen and Tony Payne, 8 studies

To the Householder
1 TIMOTHY
Authors: Phillip Jensen and Greg Clarke, 9 studie

Run the Race
2 TIMOTHY
Author: Bryson Smith, 6 studies

The Path to Godliness
TITUS
Authors: Phillip Jensen and Tony Payne, 6 studies

From Shadow to Reality
HEBREWS
Author: Joshua Ng, 10 studies

The Implanted Word
JAMES
Authors: Phillip Jensen and Kirsten Birkett, 8 studies

Homeward Bound
1 PETER
Authors: Phillip Jensen and Tony Payne, 10 studies

All You Need to Know
2 PETER
Author: Bryson Smith, 6 studies

The Vision Statement
REVELATION
Author: Greg Clarke, 9 studies

Bold I Approach
PRAYER
Author: Tony Payne, 6 studies

Cash Values
MONEY
Author: Tony Payne, 5 studies

The Blueprint
DOCTRINE
Authors: Phillip Jensen and Tony Payne, 11 studies

Woman of God
THE BIBLE ON WOMEN
Author: Terry Blowes, 8 studies